Who's Pulling My Strings?

Companion Writing Journal

A Self-Discovery Adventure

&

Journey to Becoming Free

Mardi Kirkland

BALBOA.
PRESS
A DIVISION OF HAY HOUSE

Balboa Press books may be ordered through booksellers or by contacting:

Balboa Press
A Division of Hay House
1663 Liberty Drive
Bloomington, IN 47403
www.balboapress.com
1 (877) 407-4847

ISBN: 978-1-5043-9627-1 (sc)
ISBN: 978-1-5043-9702-5 (e)

Print information available on the last page.

Balboa Press rev. date: 06/22/2018

CONTENTS

INTRODUCTION

It's an exciting time. It's a sacred time! You are embarking on a marvelous adventure – quite possibly the most exciting, and I believe the most important one of your life. People tend to think traveling and seeing the world is their greatest adventure – not necessarily so. I assure you there is nothing more *mind-blowing* than the journey inward to explore the unconscious world inside your mind – and *mind blowing* is a good description for what you want to do.

Our unconscious, unexamined thoughts and beliefs are creating the reality of our everyday life, whether we are aware of it or not. When you think about your life do you ever wonder *why* it is the way it is? Do you sometimes wish it was different? Of course – we all do. This adventure will bring light and awareness to your previously unknown *whys*. From this awareness you will be empowered to make changes and create new realities.

The fact that you have this journal in your hands is proof that you are ready to give yourself more – ready to explore and shed the thoughts, beliefs and feelings that have put limits on the quality of your life.

When you think about your life, do you say -- "my life feels good?" If not – why not? What would it take for you to say YES? What is your payoff for not feeling good? What is the quality of your life if you feel bad?

I believe it is essential to ask ourselves – is there anything more important than feeling good? Oh, some might say that sounds selfish – that life should be about being of service and helping others. Ok, that's fine – and my question back is, "what's wrong with feeling good in the process?" Also, "what is the quality of my service if I am feeling bad?"

What gets in the way of feeling good is believing we don't deserve it. If not in our conscious awareness, thoughts of unworthiness are harbored in our unconscious mind that put a governor on how much good we allow ourselves to receive.

Think of your life as a play on a theater stage. Are you playing the role of actor or do you feel like you are reacting to the events in your life? As you embark on this adventure, you will discover you are actually the *creator, writer, director* and *lead actor* of your life. If you feel more like you are a re-actor this doesn't mean you are not the *creator* -- it simply means you are an *unconscious creator.*

What motivated me to write "Who's Pulling My Strings" about the twist and turns in my journey was the hope that it would spark within you thoughts and questions about your life – that it would trigger a desire for you to embark on your own adventure of self-discovery, healing and feeling free.

This personal journal follows the theme and questions I shared in "Who's Pulling My Strings" to make it as easy for you to launch your own path of self-healing. I also want you to feel like you have me, a companion, coach and cheerleader with you on your adventurous journey.

A few things to remember a you navigate your adventure:

1. Don't edit. Feel free to write whatever comes into your mind. You're the only one who is going to read what you write. You want to discover your absolute truth.

2. Whenever you are unsure about what you are really thinking or feeling – *Play Pretend.* If you've read "Who's Pulling My Strings" you know I do this a lot. It truly is magical. Whenever you think you are just *making it up*, what comes out is easily recognized as far more your truth than fiction. *Playing Pretend* removes your resistance to knowing the truth.

3. There may be moments when you find some of the thoughts that appear feel a bit scary. I definitely had some of those moments. What I learned is that the only way to make what frightens or repels you *disappear* is to bring it forth into the light of day. The good news is that when you honestly look your thoughts in the face and acknowledge them, whatever the fear is disappears.

Ready? Let's get started!

Where Am I

and

What Do I Want?

Before you embark on a journey it helps -- actually, it is essential -- to have a clear idea of where you want to go, and to know where you are before you start. Otherwise, it is easy to get side- tracked along the way. Sometimes you might even forget where you are going.

Think of this as creating a map for yourself. Where do you want to go? Where are you now?

This can be fun and easy. Don't feel like you need to write long epistles. In fact, sometimes you may not know yet what you want or don't want. It can be easy to get bogged down and stop before you start – how well I know. So, just keep it simple.

WHAT DO I WANT?

Maybe you haven't given yourself permission to consider this before. Life is something that you think has just *happened* to you. Now, it's your turn to dream, to create, to consider that *you* are the designer of your life.

Allow yourself to *pretend.* Anything is allowed. Pretend there is a *Transformation Agent* standing in front of you, pen and paper in hand, ready to take your order for everything you would like to be present in your life.

Let's do a little dreaming about your ideal life

How do I want to feel?

Here are a few ideas to get you started -- happy, calm, successful, peaceful, loved, satisfied, good enough

_____

_____

_____

_____

_____

There are many aspects that make up the totality of your life. What do you want these **various facets of your life to look and feel like?**

Imagine your life is perfect in every respect. What would it look like?

These are the kinds of relationships I want...

_____

_____

_____

_____

My ideal work looks like this...

_____

_____

_____

_____

_____

_____

My body and health look like this...

_____

_____

_____

_____

_____

_____

My spiritual connection is...

_____

Just as a candle cannot burn without fire, men cannot live without a spiritual life.
Buddha

_____

_____

_____

_____

This is how I want to play and have fun...

_____

_____

_____

_____

_____

_____

A funny thing happens when you start thinking about what you want – it brings up all the stuff in your life that you don't want.

Where are you now? Nobody's life is perfect. It's ok to wish for aspects of your life to be other than they are.

Though no one can go back and make a brand new start, anyone can start from now and make a brand new ending. Carl Bard

THIS IS WHAT I WANT TO BE DIFFERENT

My Feelings -- like fearful, self-doubt, unloved, unhappy, wrong, relevant

If you hear a voice within you say you cannot paint, then by all means paint and that voice will be silenced.
Vincent Van Gogh

_____

_____

_____

_____

_____

_____

_____

What I don't like about my relationships…

_____

_____

_____

_____

_____

_____

_____

I don't like this about my work...

_____

_____

_____

_____

_____

I don't like this about my body, my health...

_____

_____

_____

_____

I wish this was different in my Spiritual Life...

_____

_____

_____

_____

_____

_____

My Play and Fun aren't...

_____

I am going to keep having fun every day I have left because there is no other way of life. You just have to decide whether you are a Tigger or an Eeyore. Randy Pausch

_____

_____

_____

_____

_____

_____

Now you have a clear map that shows you where you are and where you want to go.

Are you ready to explore all that's in between? I'll be with you all the way -- let's do it.

How Did I Get Here?

What's My Story?

What is my story?

Writing your story will help you to know the path – the one that's unique to you – the one you need to take.

Let's go back to the beginning of your life? How did it start? Do some reminiscing about your early childhood years? What are the pivotal moments and events in your life? Who are the major players?

This a fun project. Get the child within you to help you, and write it as a fairytale. In my experience, this made writing my story entertaining – and it kept me from getting stuck in the drama. It assisted me in seeing clearly who and what influenced me to become the me I am. I believe the same will be true for you.

Besides the fun of writing your story, it will give you a clear picture of all the players in your life. It also will help you identify the different parts of yourself that you'll want to engage.

Once upon a time...

_____

_____

The whole story is about you. You are the main character.
don Miguel Ruiz

_____

_____

_____

_____

_____

_____

_____

_____

_____

_____

_____

_____

_____

_____

_____

_____

_____

_____

Stories are the shortest distance between us and truth. So when we understand and uncover these stories, we gain the opportunity to understand maybe we need a new story.
Chris Cade

_____

_____

_____

_____

_____

_____

_____

_____

_____

_____

_____

_____

There is a surrendering to your story and then a knowing that you don't have to stay in your story.
Colette Baron Reid

_____

_____

_____

_____

_____

_____

_____

_____

_____

_____

_____

_____

_____

What Am I Thinking?

It is your thoughts about life experiences -- your perceptions of them -- that have determined your life path, not the actual events themselves. Sound shocking? It did to me at first. Let's say it another way -- your reality is created by what you are thinking.

Do you know with absolute certainty that the *events* of your life have created your life course? Or, might it possibly be your *thoughts*, the decisions you made -- your beliefs -- that have determined where your life is today?

This is exciting, for if this is true, this also means you are the *creator*. If you so desire you can choose different thoughts, different beliefs that will affect changes in your life experiences.

Your thoughts are not neutral. What does this mean? The mind automatically attaches a meaning or judgement to everything it thinks about, sees or hears.

Criticism is something that goes on in your mind all the time whether you voice it or not. Every time you look at a person, object or situation you think thoughts that put a label on what you are looking at—positive or negative.

Let's explore.

Look at objects around you and focus intently on them one at a time, shutting everything else out. Choose several items, like the chair you're sitting on, a table, desk, lamp, door – anything. If you are outside plants, trees, animals and birds are good too.

As you focus on each one, listen to the thoughts that appear in your mind about the object and write down your first thoughts. Don't edit.

_____

_____

_____

_____

_____

_____

Judging is acting on a limited knowledge. Learn the art of observing without evaluating.
Pushpa Rana

_____

_____

_____

_____

_____

_____

Do the same thing with various people – people you know well, acquaintances, and even a few strangers as well.

Close your eyes and focus on them one at a time. Write down your first thoughts about each one without editing what comes up. You'll find this especially interesting with strangers, maybe even someone you see in a grocery store. First impressions are fascinating.

_____

_____

_____

_____

*When you
judge others,
you do not
define them,
you define
yourself.*
Earl Nightingale

_____

_____

_____

_____

_____

_____

_____

_____

_____

_____

_____

_____

_____

_____

*When you judge other people
without wanting to know the
true story behind their actions, is
usually when there is something
inside of you that is so broken
that if you found out what you
believed about them was a lie,
you wouldn't want to accept it or
make amends.* Shannon Alder

Moving From Victim Thinking to Knowing I Am Creator

When things happen to you that you don't like, or when you feel criticized by what someone said about you, it is easy to feel like you are a victim of the circumstance. And yet, if you are willing to accept that your thoughts are the creator of your reality, then there must be a correlation between your thoughts, what others are saying and what's happening in your life.

Think of your life as a giant mirror of what is going on inside you. The key here is being willing to look in the mirror – with honesty. Your first glimpses may be painful, for who likes to admit that what is happening is actually coming from inside you. However, once you are able to stop resisting and accept that this is possible, you will realize the mirror is a healing gift. It allows you to see what needs to be healed inside, and in turn enables you to create a happier outside life.

You are always the creator – the question is -- are you creating consciously or un-consciously?

Let's explore some experiences and words said that were upsetting to you.

The event or the words said:

_____

_____

_____

_____

_____

How does this make me feel? Answer with "I am" statements (I feel like I am wrong, stupid, not good enough, fat, etc.).

_____

_____

After I got over the shock of learning the critics were a mirror for my own thoughts the idea became exciting. Instead of criticism being a weapon that hurt me it became the key to unlocking the door to those disturbing secrets I had hidden from myself. Who's Pulling My Strings

_____

_____

_____

_____

When was the first time I remember feeling this way? Go back as far as you can remember. It will almost always be something that happened when you were a child.

_____

_____

_____

_____

What are some other times between then and now that I felt this way?

_____

_____

_____

_____

_____

_____

_____

_____

_____

_____

That was then – what am I still telling myself now? Remember to use "I am" statements.

_____

I never thought I was a Bully… until I listened to how I spoke to myself. I think I owe myself an apology. Anita Opper

_____

_____

_____

_____

_____

When you listen to the monologue about you running in your mind, you will most likely find you are hearing what you started believing about you when you were a child. Now that you know it – you can do something about it.

Here is the truth I am ready to hear me say about me

I am perfect just the way I am

_____

I am beautiful

_____

I am lovable

_____

I am kind

_____

I am smart

_____

I am worthy of goodness

_____

Discovering

My

BIG Lie

Everyone has one – it is your *core negative belief* about you. It is a lie. Always, always, always a lie. Your big lie is typically a secret – a secret you keep from yourself. Why? Because it is painful. It feels unbearable. We use denial to protect ourselves.

This *core negative belief* is the source of every other negative thought and belief you have about you.

It's like the hand holding many strings connected to balloons.

You may be asking, "Why do I want to uncover this secret if it is painful?"

You do want to know and expose this lie. It is creating unhappiness everywhere in your life and you don't know why. If you don't know the cause how can you do anything to change it?

It is amazingly easy to discover this BIG lie, the most negative belief you have about you. While a part of you has been intent on keeping it a secret, there is also a part that is longing for you to know and stop the lie – to bring in a positive feeling of love.

On the next page fill in every line with the first thought that enters your mind. Yes, repeat the process until you fill the page.

You will find that some I AM statements are written more than once. There will undoubtedly be one that is repeated more than any others. It will become obvious to you, and not just because you see it written on the page. You will feel it in your body.

My Most Negative Thought About Me Is . . .

I AM _____

I AM _____

I AM _____

I AM _____

I AM _____

I AM _____

I AM _____

I AM _____

I AM _____

I AM _____

I AM _____

I AM _____

I AM _____

I AM _____

I AM _____

MY BIG LIE IS . . . I AM _____

Breathe

How do you act out your BIG LIE?

There are two different ways we act out our BIG LIE. Some of us literally *act it out,* while others do everything possible to *hide* it.

You will always have one way that is dominant even though in varying situations you may show up *acting it out,* and other times you will find yourself doing everything possible to *hide it.* Since you are unconscious of the fact that you have this BIG LIE, it will show up in every arena of your life without your even knowing it.

If you are someone who *acts it out,* it is like picking up a chair and walking around holding it out in front of you saying, "See my chair? This is my chair. Look at my chair, everybody."

Are you the *hide it* person? If you are you will do everything possible to attempt to keep it invisible. You'll hook your foot around the leg of the chair and drag it behind you saying, "Look at me? No, there's nothing behind me. Aren't I wonderful? Look at me. Aren't I great?"

(Circle One)
The way I most act out my BIG LIE is . . .   *I act it out*   *I hide it*

Some ways I act out my BIG LIE are . . .

_____

_____

_____

_____

_____

_____

_____

_____

_____

I am trying to hide my BIG LIE when I . . .

_____

_____

_____

_____

_____

_____

_____

Finding the Thinker

Inside Me

You have uncovered your BIG LIE. Now, let's get to know the *you* who first told you this lie and believed it. Knowing this *you* will make it possible to unravel the story you told yourself, and begin to know the truth and beauty that is you.

Be patient. This part of you, along with the BIG LIE, has been deeply buried and well-hidden all of your life. Sometimes it takes some sleuthing to bring her up to the surface and out in the open. Use the mirror of others critical, unkind words and unpleasant life events. As awful as they may feel -- they play a magical role in uncovering what is hidden.

You may find it challenging in the beginning to find the corresponding thoughts these words and events are mirroring. That's ok – you'll get there. The more you have denied the negative thoughts, the deeper you have buried them -- hoping you would never find them.

This is another good time to *play pretend*. It is non-threatening, and is the easiest way I have found to get beyond denial. It works.

Write the story of an event that upset you -- the "He said," "She said," "This happened."

Life is the movie you see through your own unique eyes. It makes little difference what's happening out there. It's how you take it that counts.

Dennis Waitley

Again, playing pretend, ask, "If this thought is inside me what does it look like?" Write down your first thoughts no matter how strange they may sound to you.

_____

_____

_____

_____

Where inside my mind might I already be thinking these thoughts? In other words, "what thoughts about me are these words or this event mirroring?"

_____

_____

_____

_____

Since you are just *playing pretend* you can feel safe to write it down. Until you acknowledge and write down your first thoughts, there is no space for more to come in.
Read over what you have written, and as you do, notice where you are feeling it in your body.

What physical sensations might you be experiencing?

Is there an ache in your heart?

A sickening feeling in the pit of your stomach?

Maybe a tightness in your neck and shoulders?

I feel _____

_____

_____

_____

_____

If you are at all like me some beliefs may make you may feel nauseous when you first become aware of them. This is a time that I recommend you summon your courage, and allow yourself to really feel whatever awfulness comes up. It truly won't last long.

It is *feeling the feelings* that will take you where you need to go and speed your healing -- make you able to change this erroneous belief you made up.

Now it is time to ask, "When was the first time I had this thought and felt these feelings?" "How old was the child who first thought this?" You may feel like you are hearing the voices of others inside your head – your parents, teachers, friends.

It takes courage … to endure the sharp pains of self-discovery rather than choose to take the dull pain of unconsciousness that would last the rest of our lives. —— Marianne Williamson

To be able to change this erroneous belief you made up, you have to find the "me" that repeated their words and formed the belief.

Become the observer. Start with current time when an event or someone's words upset you. It doesn't feel good when . . .

_____

_____

_____

_____

_____

How old was I when I first thought this thought? _____

Who else's words am I hearing? _____

Imagine you are rising above your life and looking down – taking a cosmic viewpoint of your life. From this perspective, again playing pretend – ask,

"What must a person believe about themselves to be bothered by this event/these words?"

Use "I am" statements.

_____

_____

_____

_____

_____

_____

This is a sacred time – a healing time for you. Don't be in a hurry, and don't approach it as a project to be accomplished in a set amount of time. This is a process – and it may go on for quite awhile.

Breathe

Now, let's travel back through your life. Take time to observe along the way the different times and ways you've played out this belief.

Ways I've acted out this belief...

_____

_____

_____

_____

_____

_____

Keep going until you get to the very first time you thought the thoughts and formed the belief.

Bring your awareness down into this child that is you. Become her totally. Feel what she is feeling.

My child is feeling _____

_____

_____

_____

_____

Still feeling this child's pain – become the loving parent. Have a conversation with her.

Tell her how much you love her -- how wonderful she is.

As you are writing what you want to say to your child, you may be surprised to find that the child in you is wanting to talk with you as well. In fact you may have a very interesting and revealing dialogue going back and forth between you.

If you find this happening, don't freak out. Welcome it. This is a good thing. The child in you needs and deserves to be heard – this is a big step in your healing.

Words from my child _____

_____

Often the inner child holds information and feelings for the adult. Some of these feelings are painful; others are actually fun. The child holds the playfulness and innocence the adult has had to bury. Laura Davis

---

Tell your child you are going to talk about the story she made up -- that you are going to help her learn that it is not true.

Talk with your child about what is true about her.

We nurture our creativity when we release our inner child. Let it run and roam free. It will take you on a brighter journey.
Serina Hartwell

_____

_____

_____

Make a commitment to spend time every day with your child, even if it is only two or three minutes.

Check in at the end of the day – to see how she feels about the day. It is important to talk about the good things that happened, and even more necessary if someone said or did something that was upsetting. Be sure you talk with her to get her take on the day.

What happened today . . .

_____

_____

_____

_____

_____

_____

How is your child feeling about it?

_____

_____

_____

_____

_____

_____

_____

_____

How might I and my child look at what happened differently?

_____

_____

_____

_____

_____

_____

_____

_____

_____

_____

_____

_____

What Do I Do With These Feelings?

As you spend time talking with your child, you might begin to feel sensations that in present time are unfamiliar, yet bring a sense, a faint remembrance, of something familiar from a distant past. When this happens, you are making a connection with the part of you that didn't feel good about you -- the little child in you that made up stories about how bad or ugly or unworthy you were.

As a child, accompanying these made up stories about yourself were feelings you felt in your body. As scary as these feelings are -- that you are feeling them now is a very good thing.

If your thoughts are what *create* your reality -- your *feelings* are the fuel that burns to bring your *creations* into form. Your feelings beg to be acknowledged. Feelings are energy, and energy is always in motion. Once you feel and express them, feelings are released. The energy within and around you can then begin to flow freely. Fantastic.

It isn't necessary to act out your feelings (in many cases probably not the best idea either) – you do need to feel them in order to become free of their control over you and your life.

Unexpressed feelings become bottled up energy inside you. If your life is feeling stagnant, this may be why – the energy can't flow

Sometimes, when a negative feeling is in the forefront of your consciousness, it feels very intense – even frightening. You may even have the sickening thought that you're going to feel this way forever.

When this happens to me, it helps to think of my life as a glass of water that has *mud* (negative feelings) in the bottom. The only way to get the sludge out is to stir it to bring it up to the surface -- feel it -- to flush it out.

Whenever you go into the mud, it helps to remind yourself that you are completely safe.

Feeling your feelings won't kill you. Feelings can't hurt you. Not feeling your feelings just might.

The truth is the intensity of the negative feelings only lasts a short time. What is really cool, is that the release of negative feelings creates a vacuum. A vacuum demands to be filled, so you have the opportunity to fill it with a feeling of your choice – like more of your true, loving essence.

Schedule an appointment with yourself – call it your Emotional Healing appointment. 30 minutes is a good length. This is a time to practice feeling – the deep defenseless feelings that you want to release.

This won't necessarily be easy at first as you've spent a lifetime avoiding feeling them. I promise it gets easier and easier, because the relief you feel after letting go of the pain and the weight of them is something you want to experience more and more.

From the list of Deep Defenseless Feelings below, choose first the one that stands out as most familiar (it may be a different one each time you do it).

Say the word, and imagine the feeling. It helps to drop your head, as if looking down, and close your eyes. Looking down helps you access your emotional body, and closing your eyes will shut out distractions.

Play pretend – pretend you know how it feels. It can help to pretend you are an actor playing a role where this feeling is required. This will get your mind out of the way.

Deep Defenseless Feelings

Abandoned	*Humiliated*
Alone	*Hurt*
Anguish	*Loneliness*
Embarrassed	*Feeling Lost*
Fatigue	*Rejected*
Fear	*Self-loathing*
Grief	*Sadness*
Helpless	*Shame*
Horror	*Terror*

Ready? Look down. Close your eyes and imagine the feeling.

You may pop out of the feeling after only a few seconds. That's ok. Be willing to do it again, and again, and again.

Imagine you, the actor, are in front of the director, and you want to be able to go deeper and deeper into the feeling. You want to make him feel what you are feeling.

After repeating this feeling as many times as you can, stop -- become aware of how you are feeling now. Most likely, you will feel a lightness, a buoyancy that wasn't there before.

Take a few minutes and write about your experience.

I am feeling _____

_____

_____

_____

_____

Each time you practice and experience a release of a negative feeling, you create space within – a vacuum. A vacuum will always attract something to fill itself, so this is a rich time for you to fill the vacuum with a feeling of your choosing.

Don't be in a hurry to leave a practice without taking this time to bring in what you want. This is why you have scheduled 30 minutes. Look at this practice as creating a vacuum – then filling the vacuum.

Here are some "feel good" words to use as a guide.

Feeling Good

Love	*Relief*
Awe	*Happiness*
Carefree	*Joy*
Contentment	*Mastery*
Ecstasy/Bliss	*Peace*
Gratitude	*Wonder*

Use the same process as with the first practice when you dropped into negative feelings. Close your eyes and look down – pretend you are an actor, and you want the imaginary director sitting in front of you to feel as good you are feeling.

No rushing here – spend as much time dropping into the good feelings as you did with the feelings of pain.

Take some time and write about how you are feeling now.

I am Feeling _____

_____

_____

_____

_____

_____

_____

_____

Breathe

Calling Up

My

Courage

You are doing great. Let's pause for a few moments -- acknowledge you and the child within for the connection you've made, and the communication that is beginning to flow between you.

It takes courage to do this exploration. Courage to be totally honest with you. Courage to delve deep and clean out the debris. Maybe you are afraid of what you might find. It is like a mystery adventure – exciting and sometimes scary.

Vulnerability is our most accurate measurement of courage. Brene Brown

Are you feeling tempted at this point to tell yourself, "this is good, but maybe far enough?" The mind starts creating excuses why you should maybe stop the journey here. These are some I used: "I don't have time to do this. I've got to get this project done for work." Or, "I've got to get together with these friends I haven't seen for awhile."

What are yours? Let's get these excuses out of your mind and on to the page.

Excuse #1 _____

Excuse #2 _____

Excuse #3 _____

Excuse #4 _____

Excuse #5 _____

Take a few deep breaths. Try breathing in through your nose, hold it for a few seconds, and breathe out through your mouth. A few more times. Ah - that feels much, much better.

Breathe!

At this point it is helpful to ask yourself, "How motivated am I to walk the healing path?" There is not a good or bad, right or wrong answer. It is a good time to be completely honest with yourself and know your level of commitment to you.

Here are a few questions to ask:

On a scale of 1 to 10 how happy am I with my life right now?

_____

_____

_____

_____

How free am I feeling to be totally me?

*The first step
toward change
is acceptance.
Once you accept
yourself, you
open the door to
change.*
    Will Garcia

_____

_____

_____

_____

_____

*Who do I believe I **really** am?*

_____

_____

_____

_____

How much of who I think I am is dictated by what I think others want or expect me to be?

_____

_____

_____

_____

_____

On a scale of 1 to 10 what is my level of courage and commitment to be completely honest with myself -- no matter what arises that I don't want to see -- and stay the course?

_____

_____

_____

_____

What kind of legacy do I want to pass on? What mark do I want to leave on the world?

_____   *Choosing to*

_____   *exercise the*

_____   *courage to take*
                                             this journey is not
_____   *only going to*
                                             change the course
_____   *of your life.*
                                             It will affect the
_____   *lives of everyone*
                                             that is important
_____   *to you.*

When you look at it this way is there any other option for you but to go all the way?

You are embarking on a journey of discovery and reclaiming your true self. And it does take courage. Sometimes, it takes a lot of it.

You're doing great! Let's keep going.

Meeting &

Transforming My

Protector

When we were children, we created a *Protector* in our mind, thinking we needed it to keep us safe. The *Protector* took on the role of fearful, judging parent whose job was to protect us from what it defined as harm, and to keep us under control.

This theory was introduced to me in an enlightening book entitled, "Embracing Ourselves," about a healing tool called *Voice Dialogue*. Getting acquainted with the *Protector* was most helpful while dealing with the excuses and resistance to going forward in my healing journey.

In my life, it seems, the *Protector's* job was to judge and condemn me if it deemed I was out of control, before the *big people* could harm the child.

I recommend getting to know the *Protector* in you, and establishing a healthy relationship with this fearful, protective part of your mind. It makes this journey so much easier. My *Protector* and I needed to talk -- and we did – a lot.

Are you concerned about having conversations with different parts of yourself? No – you are not what psychologists call a *multiple personality*. Who you are is the sum total of all the aspects of you, at every age. You are a multi-dimensional being, and your *Protector* has played a huge role in your life up until now.

To help you get started I find it helpful to place an empty chair opposite you representing the *Protector*. Try it. Whenever you want to access and speak as the *Protector*, move to that chair.

Not sure how to get the conversation started? Here's a snippet of one conversation I had that was very beneficial. I share it to give you the idea. My voice as the adult Mardi is "M" and the *Protector* is "P."

M-   *I really want to talk to you, Protector. I am just beginning to realize that you have had an important role in my life and I want to get to know you.*

P-   *You do? That's good. I have worked hard for you. I've always wanted to keep you safe, and sometimes that hasn't been easy. Sometimes you take chances that scare me.*

M-   *Tell me about this. How have I frightened you?*

P-   *Well, my job is to monitor everything you say or do, and try to keep you from getting into trouble. Sometimes you want to say or do things that I know others won't like. I try to stop you, but sometimes you don't listen to me, and you do it anyway. That's a terrifying time. I want everyone to like you. I want you to be loved. I don't want you to go to hell.*

M-   *Is that what you think will happen -- that I will go to hell?*

P-   *Well yes, of course. You have to do what they want you to do or you're bad. If you're bad it means God won't love you, and if God doesn't love you, you will go to hell. My job is exhausting.*

M-   *Wow! I didn't even know you existed, let alone that you had such an important role in my life. I acknowledge you. You've done a great job.*

P-   *Thank you.*

Got the idea? Now it's your turn. When you feel your conversation is complete, it is important that you and your *Protector* create a new position within you with a new title and new job description. Mine became the *Thought Detector.*

When you make friends with your *Protector,* and together transform it into its new title and position, the journey will become much easier. You will never again feel like you are alone – you will have an ally beside you.

Have fun with this. This is important and effective work you are doing.

_____

_____

_____

Releasing the Feelings

That Don't

Feel Good

When you start this process of releasing negative feelings, don't expect to do the exercise once and be done with your anger, sadness or shame. We have been burying these feelings for a lifetime, and it may take the rest of our lives to release them all. I am constantly reminding myself to be patient, "I'm not walking on water, yet."

Do your best to allow yourself to sink deeply into the feeling, like you practiced in Section 7. Sometimes it feels more like wallowing. You've been holding these feelings inside for a long time, probably most of your life. It has taken a lot of your energy to keep them buried.

You may be asking, "Why do I want to bring forth these long-buried feelings, and why do you recommend it's a good thing to do?"

Reminding you again -- you want to feel them because feeling them is the key to their release -- the only path to living free.

Sometimes, when an event happens or words are said that trigger negative feelings arising, the temptation is to want to feel the feelings and react in the moment. However, at the moment this may not be an appropriate action.

As soon as possible, set aside time and space, to feel and to examine what the event or words activated inside you.

Shoving the feelings under the rug will never allow you to experience the freedom and joy you desire.

As you start this section on releasing feelings, do it in the order given here. Here's why.

Anger is the feeling we hold closest to the surface. We use anger to mask what's underneath -- our hurt and sadness. Then, below the anger, the hurt and sadness is the feeling of shame – our rejection of our very beingness.

Breathe

Releasing

My

Anger

You may think you are never angry – or, you may have angry feelings about a lot of things. It doesn't matter. Start by being willing to explore the anger you may or may not be aware is inside you. If you are someone who believes you are never angry – trust me – you may be one who has more buried inside than someone who often explodes with anger.

I am one who was in denial, even boasted that I was never angry. Then, one day I experienced not only was I angry, I was full of rage to the point I thought I might never feel love again. It was tempting to *stuff* the rage and pretend I was beyond it –but peace and love cannot co-exist with anger and rage.

Time to Get Physical

Getting physical and moving your body is one of the best ways to get anger up and out of you. It helps to break it loose and get the energy flowing. This may seem daunting at first, and like you are going off the deep end. Start slowly until you learn that you can trust the process.

Find a place and time where you can be alone, and, if possible, make noise without disturbing anyone. Insure you have plenty of time afterwards to process the thoughts and feelings you'll be activating. Have this journal and a pen nearby to write down any memories that surface.

One thing you can be sure of – you will feel light and peace on the other side of an anger release.

Here are several ideas for *getting physical*. Choose the one that you feel will work best for you in your surroundings.

Important: Remember to keep breathing while you are in the process. Breathing really helps you to let go.

- *Kneel on the floor with a pillow or two in front of you that you can beat on with an object. While pounding on the pillow, shout out loud over and over, "I am so angry, I am so angry, I am so angry." Do this until you feel the energy of your anger flowing through your body.*

- *Throw a Temper Tantrum. Stand in one place and stomp your feet like a child, again saying over and over, "I am so angry, I am so angry, I am so angry."*

- *Sit in your car, (while it is parked of course) an option when you are challenged to make sure no one can hear you shout. You can't get much body movement in the car, but it is a safe place to yell your head off. Again, "I am so angry, I am so angry, I am so angry."*

These are my feelings, thoughts and memories that came up

_____

_____

_____

_____

_____

_____

*It's not what's in
front of you that
blocks your
way…it's what's
inside of you that
holds you back.*
Robin Williams as Mork

_____

_____

_____

_____

_____

_____

_____

_____

_____

_____

_____

What's the Real Reason I Feel Angry?

There are two lessons in a course called "A Course In Miracles" that I believe are invaluable to understanding what is happening when words and events trigger our emotions.

- "I AM NEVER UPSET FOR THE REASON I THINK." It doesn't say *sometimes* or *occasionally*, it says *never*.

- I am upset because "I AM SEEING ONLY THE PAST."

Try testing these theories. Ask yourself how a current situation that is bothering you might be like something from your past -- kind of like a déjà vu experience.

A Present irritation ⎯⎯⎯⎯⎯⎯⎯⎯⎯⎯⎯⎯⎯⎯⎯⎯⎯⎯

_____

_____

_____

_____

This is how it reminds me of something in my past _____

_____

_____

_____

_____

_____

Nothing ever goes away until it has taught us what we need to know.

Pema Chodron

Using the Little Things That Irritate Me

Driving your car is a time when it is easy to feel irritated. If someone cuts in front of you, do you feel shoved back and unimportant? Just as a child, do you feel like you don't matter?

Are you annoyed when someone in front of you is driving too slowly, and you can't get around them?

Whenever irritating driving experiences happen, express your anger -- out loud. Allow yourself to remember times in your past when you felt this way.

Ask, "When was the first time I felt this way?" You may remember a time when you felt you were being stopped from doing what you wanted, or from going where you wanted to go. You felt powerless.

Driving Irritation _____

_____

_____

_____

This is how it made me feel _____

_____

_____

_____

_____

As you are remembering other times you felt this, ask "When was the first time I felt this way?"

_____

_____

_____

_____

STOP *– feel the feelings -- let them release. You have now created more space within.*

Now, fill this space with feelings of your choosing. Use the list below as a guide.

Love	*Happiness*
Awe	*Joy*
Carefree	*Mastery*
Contentment	*Relief*
Ecstasy or Bliss	*Peace*
Gratitude	*Wonder*

When I fill this space with _____ (good feeling), I feel...

_____

_____

_____

_____

_____

_____

_____

_____

Feeling Sadness

&

Mourning My Losses

Once you experience releasing some of the layers of anger you've been holding on to, you are able to realize it has been a cover up for something deeper – feelings of sadness, disappointment and regrets you have denied. This isn't about the profound grief that comes with the loss of a loved one. This is about everyday life happenings.

How many times has something happened that caused you to feel hurt, and you grit your teeth and went on, pretending nothing happened? The sad thing is that when you do that, you also -- usually unconsciously -- tell yourself a negative story about you.

Regardless of the cause it is essential to allow yourself to feel your sorrow about events in your life that resulted in disappointment rather than joy. Your unfelt grief causes you to keep a lock on the door to your heart.

The truth is your life fully lived will always have its share of disappointments as well as victories. If you don't take a chance on something that might bring you loss, you will greatly limit your opportunities to experience the joy of triumph and success.

The tricky part is to not sit in a place of judgment about the events of your life that you wish hadn't happened -- to not live in regret about what you wish had been and wasn't.

"You might never fail on the scale I did, but it is impossible to live without failing at something, unless you live so cautiously that you might as well not have lived at all—in which case, you fail by default."
Harry Potter author, J.K. Rowling. The first 12 publishers rejected her manuscript

When you look honestly at your life, you will undoubtedly find it full of *I should haves,* and *if onlys.* Judging our lives seems to be a component of the human condition. "I *should* have done better, known better, it *should not* have happened that way. *If only* my mother had loved me differently. *If only* my father hadn't left. *If only* I had married a good man instead of a loser." The list is endless.

When you are invested in regret, you enroll yourself in victimhood. You believe it is someone else's fault your life hasn't turned out the way you wanted it to be. Or, you judge and condemn yourself because of things you said or did, and that hurts.

Letting go of sadness and regret isn't as difficult as you might think. It actually feels good to feel the pain and let it go. And, it allows you to create a new path.

Time to get started!

The first step is becoming aware and looking honestly at your "shoulds" and "if onlys." There are 4 steps:

1. *Make a list of your "shoulds" and "if onlys." Call them a Judgment.*

2. *Next to each one, write down how it made you feel about you.*

3. *Speak the feeling out loud and take a few minutes to drop into it feeling it as deeply as you can.*

4. *See the situation again and look for a different perspective – one that includes acceptance without judgment. Here is an example:*

> **Judgment**: I should never have married the man. If I had only been wiser I would have known it was a mistake from the start.

> **Acceptance**: I see now that marrying him was meant to be since the way he treated me was a perfect reflection of what I thought of myself at the time.

Knowing that we all have a plethora of *shoulds* and *if onlys*, I am providing you space here to record and turn around many judgments.

My Judgment   *How it makes me feel*

_____   _____

Feel the feeling

My New Perspective of Acceptance

_____

_____

_____

My Judgment   *How it makes me feel*

_____   _____

Feel the feeling

My New Perspective of Acceptance

_____

_____

_____

My Judgment   *How it makes me feel*

_____   _____

Feel the feeling

My New Perspective of Acceptance

_____

_____

_____

My Judgment   *How it makes me feel*

_____   _____

Feel the feeling

My New Perspective of Acceptance

_____

_____

_____

My Judgment   *How it makes me feel*

_____   _____

Feel the feeling

My New Perspective of Acceptance

_____

_____

_____

My Judgment   *How it makes me feel*

_____   _____

Feel the feeling

My New Perspective of Acceptance

_____

_____

_____

My Judgment   *How it makes me feel*

_____   _____

Feel the feeling

My New Perspective of Acceptance

_____

_____

_____

My Judgment   *How it makes me feel*

_____   _____

Feel the feeling

My New Perspective of Acceptance

_____

_____

_____

My Judgment   *How it makes me feel*

_____   _____

Feel the feeling

My New Perspective of Acceptance

_____

_____

_____

My Judgment   *How it makes me feel*

_____   _____

Feel the feeling

My New Perspective of Acceptance

_____

_____

_____

My Judgment   *How it makes me feel*

_____   _____

Feel the feeling

My New Perspective of Acceptance

_____

_____

_____

My Judgment   *How it makes me feel*

_____   _____

Feel the feeling

My New Perspective of Acceptance

_____

_____

_____

Breathe

What stories do I tell to avoid my feelings?

Another *Human Condition* factor is getting caught up in our dramas. We tend to *get off* on telling our juicy stories. You know, the "You won't believe what happened to me" scenario. "He said this, he did that to me, I was this and she just didn't care." Or, "My boss doesn't appreciate me, I think she's jealous of me, I'm not being treated fairly." Blah, Blah, Blah, Blah. It is so easy to do. We've all done it – a lot. It is comparable to wearing your misery on your sleeve like a badge you've earned.

Here's the truth about telling your stories -- when you get a charge from telling everyone your dramas, it is a way of conning yourself. You think that if you are telling your story you are dealing with it. This could not be farther from the truth.

What is really happening when you choose to tell your story over and over to whomever will listen is you are staying in a place that is toxic – for you and for the people who agree to play the audience for you to share your drama.

I'm not saying you'll never get caught up in your drama and tell stories again. Of course you will – I do too. But, now you know what you are doing, and can catch yourself and stop.

Discover what you are really feeling – and, let it go.

What to do when you catch yourself caught up in a story:

One of my stories I tell is _____

_____

_____

_____   *You leave old habits behind by starting out with the thought, "I release the need for this in my life.* Wayne Dyer

_____

_____

_____

_____

_____

_____

_____

_____

_____

_____

_____

_____

How it makes me feel about me is _____

_____

_____

_____

_____

Feel the feeling – sit with it for a few moments -- let it go.

Feel the new space, the vacuum, that is now here.

Bring love, light and self-acceptance into yourself. Bask in the glow.

Love and Self-acceptance feels _____

_____

_____

_____

_____

_____

_____

_____

The first step
toward change is
acceptance. Once
you accept yourself,
you open the door
to change. Will Garcia

_____

_____

_____

_____

_____

_____

_____

_____

_____

_____

_____

I Am Ready To Let Go of Shame

So, what exactly is shame? Shame is judging the very essence of who and what you are -- your being -- to be unacceptable. Don't confuse shame with guilt. Guilt is what you feel when you judge something you have done. Shame is about your very beingness.

The Webster Dictionary defines shame as, "a condition of humiliating disgrace or disrepute, dishonor, derision, contempt."

Could there be anything worse than feeling that you are unacceptable? Unacceptable to yourself? Unacceptable to others? Unacceptable to what you know as God? I can conceive of nothing worse.

I believe that shame is to our psyche what a severed spinal cord is to the body. It paralyzes. Feelings of shame are unbearable, and we will do anything possible to avoid feeling them. And, then, we're stuck. We might as well be paralyzed.

In our society it is pretty much impossible to escape feelings of shame at least to some degree. We've all heard, "You should be ashamed of yourself," or "I'm ashamed of you." We even say it to ourselves… "I am so ashamed of myself."

This experiment will give clarity to the effect shame has on you:

Picture a little child, not necessarily you, any child.

See this child standing up straight, maybe even looking happy and smiling.

What do you see?

_____

_____

_____

_____

_____

Someone walks up to the child, and starts criticizing and ridiculing it, maybe even telling the child it is bad.

What do you see happening to the child?

What happens to its posture?

_____

_____

_____

_____

Now you know what shame feels like – and even looks like. Even though we may not show on the outside that we are shrinking and crumbling, it is how we are feeling on the inside.

When do you remember feeling shame? Begin with your childhood – perhaps when there were times other kids made fun of you and you felt criticized and ridiculed. Or, when you were told you did something wrong.

_____

_____

_____

_____

_____

Shame is the intensely painful feeling that we are unworthy of Love.
Brene Brown

_____

_____

_____

_____

_____

_____

_____

_____

_____

Set aside some time each day to feel the shame attached to one of the above experiences. Feeling it makes it possible to release it.

Now, play the role of a loving parent, and give yourself the love and acceptance needed in place of the feelings of shame.

The words I want to hear are _____

_____

_____

_____

_____

_____

_____

_____

No matter how much I get done, or is left undone, I AM ENOUGH.
Brene Brown

Stay with each experience until your feelings about it are neutral.

After each release of feelings of shame, fill the vacuum it left with love and light. Enjoy and bathe in the light of love that is now available.

Describe the feeling of love and light flowing in and through your body

_____

_____

_____

_____

_____

One new perception,
One fresh thought,
One act of surrender,
One change of heart,
One leap of faith,
Can change your life forever.
Robert Holden

_____

_____

_____

_____

Breathe

Freeing My Resistance To Change

Think about making a change in your life -- what are the first thoughts that pop up in your mind? Big or small, it doesn't matter. Do you feel resistance, or excitement? Maybe you feel a little of both. Let's do some exploration on the resistance factor.

Many people do resist change. Most likely this is based on fear. We may not want to admit we feel fear. Most of us don't. So often when talking with people about making changes, I hear, "Not me, I'm not afraid, I just don't want to." Or, "I don't see the need for it. My life is pretty good the way it is." Meanwhile, it's obvious they are miserable.

You have just been doing a lot of excavating of long held feelings. It is natural to feel a bit of fear and resistance to letting go of something that's been a part of you for most or all of your life.

When you understand why you fear and resist change, it is easier to make the decision to go forward in spite of your fears.

Let's explore your thoughts about change. Write down the first thoughts that come in your mind at the suggestion of change:

_____

_____

_____

Stop being afraid of what could go wrong, and start getting excited about what could go right.
Tony Robbins

_____

_____

_____

_____

_____

_____

_____

_____

Our beliefs about change are formed from our life experiences. The first change we encountered was when we left the womb and emerged into the world. It is very likely that our beliefs about change have a lot to do with our birth experience. Sound crazy? Trust me -- let's play with this and see what comes up for you.

Write the story of your birth. If you don't know anything about it, play pretend and imagine what you think it was like.

_____

_____

_____

_____

_____

_____

_____

_____

_____

_____

_____

What decisions do you see you may have made about change as a result of what you experienced at your birth?

_____

_____

Are you ready to release your fearful beliefs and resistance to change?

Let's create a new set of beliefs about change that will serve you. Here are some suggestions:

--Change is easy for me.
--I am free of resistance to change
--I welcome change as an opportunity to grow
--I always receive the support I need in times of change
--Change brings new good into my life

Make your new beliefs about change as general as they need to be for you to be able to actually believe and embrace them. You don't want to raise the gradient so high that it increases your fear and resistance. If you are having difficulty with this start with using the words, "I am willing" in front of your new beliefs about change.

My new beliefs about change are:

What Motivates Me?

Is it

Fear or Love?

You've explored how resistance to change is most likely connected to fear. Now let's take a look at fear as a motivator. Whenever you are tempted to stop and abort the journey forward, becoming clear about your motivating factor greatly aids in bringing you to a place of clarity.

"The Course in Miracles" teaches there are only two basic emotions: *Love* and *Fear*. No more, no less -- just *Love* and *Fear*. It is impossible for them to co-exist simultaneously. Reducing motivation down to just two factors makes it easy to understand, and to feel what is going on within you.

I believe it makes this journey to love so much more clear and simple -- especially, when you're tempted to stop and not go forward. You don't have to be sold on this premise. Just be willing to say, "What if...?"

Once you become aware of how much of the time *fear* is the motivating factor for your actions, the decision to change becomes non-negotiable. I didn't want *fear* to be the major motivator for my life, and I am certain you feel the same way.

What the ego doesn't want us to see is that our pain doesn't come from the love we weren't given in the past, but from the love we ourselves aren't giving in the present.
Marianne Williamson

Make the choice to become conscious of the source of motivation for your thoughts and actions, knowing it is either **love** or **fear.**

Here is the formula:
1. *Go back through your thoughts and actions of the day. Recapture your thoughts, words, and actions. Write down the events.*

2. *Take some time to reflect on these and ask yourself, "Was I coming from a place of love or fear?" If you are unable to honestly say you were in a place of love you'll know the only other answer is fear.*

3. *What caused the feeling of fear? Most often you will find it is a fear of some kind of loss or lack.*

4. *When the answer is fear, ask yourself what the thought or action would have been if the motivating factor had been love.*

The Event _____

_____

_____

_____

_____

_____

_____

My Motivating factor - Love or Fear? _____

What was the fear that caused my action/reaction? _____

_____

_____

_____

_____

What would my thought or action have been if love had been the motivating factor?

_____

_____

_____

_____

The Event _____

_____

_____

Love is what we were born with. Fear is what we learned here. The spiritual journey is the relinquishment, or unlearning, of fear and the acceptance of love back into our hearts."— Marianne Williamson

_____

_____

_____

My Motivating factor - Love or Fear? _____

What was the fear that caused my action/reaction? _____

_____

_____

_____

_____

What would my thought or action have been if love had been the motivating factor?

_____

_____

_____

_____

_____

The Event _____

_____

_____

_____

_____

_____

_____

My Motivating factor - Love or Fear? _____

What was the fear that caused my action/reaction? _____

What you love, you　　_____
empower
And what you　　　　_____
fear, you empower
And what you　　　　_____
empower, you
attract.　　　　　　_____
~ Author Unknown ~
　　　　　　　　　_____

What would my thought or action have been if love had been the motivating factor?

_____

_____

_____

_____

The Event _____

_____

_____

_____

_____

_____

_____

My Motivating factor - Love or Fear? _____

What was the fear that caused my action/reaction? _____

_____

_____

_____

_____

What would my thought or action have been if love had been the motivating factor?

_____

_____

_____

_____

_____

Dedicate yourself to Love. Decide to let Love be your intention, your purpose, and your point. And then let Love inspire you, support you and guide you in every other dedication you make thereafter."– Robert Holden

Remember, anything and everything from your past is treatable and curable. However, left unheeded it can keep you from being fully alive. You may be walking on earth in a body, but are you really living?

If you went to the doctor and found out you had cancer and it was curable with aggressive treatment, what would your answer be? Undoubtedly, you would say, "Let's go for it." Do you see this kind of healing work is no different? -- except there are no negative side effects to the treatment. So, "go for it!"

Re-writing My Script

Having made it this far, you *know* that you are – and always have been – the *Decision Maker*. You are the *Thinker*. You are the *Creator*. As the *Decision Maker* you are empowered to discard and change any decisions and beliefs running your life that no longer serve you. You can choose to think new thoughts, and feel the good feelings that accompany them.

ALERT: This does not give you permission to judge yourself when you fall into old habits and patterns! When you start doing the work to clean up your life, it is so easy to do this. I have been doing this work for over twenty years now, and sometimes still find myself tending to judge harshly when an old pattern of behavior pops up.

This is a Journey to Love you are on.
Self-acceptance, whatever state of mind
you may be in, is your destination.
Be gentle. Be kind to you.

The first step in re-scripting is becoming aware of the old thoughts and programming that need to be cleaned out. Just because you know something intellectually doesn't mean you have integrated it into all of your being.

Second, ask yourself the question, "How do I know this -- intellectually or experientially?" The body cannot lie, and you will feel the truth immediately.

Let's go back again to your birth story where your programming began and your first beliefs were formed. What happens to us between our birth and age 5 pretty much establishes the foundation for what follows.

Write down the events you remember during your early childhood. If there are significant memories from your birth experience, include them too. Then write down the beliefs about life you made as a result.

If you are saying, "I have no idea what I was thinking," invoke your imagination. Approach it as play, rather than a serious project. Play pretend and make up a story as if it is about someone else.

The event and my thoughts about it _____

_____

_____

_____

_____

_____

_____

What decisions did I make about myself and life as a result?

_____

_____

_____

_____

_____

_____

_____

The event and my thoughts about it _____

_____

_____

_____

_____

_____

_____

What decisions did I make about myself and life as a result?

_____

It's not whether you get knocked down, It's whether you get up. Vince Lombardi

_____

_____

_____

_____

_____

The event and my thoughts about it _____

_____

_____

_____

_____

_____

_____

What decisions did I make about myself and life as a result?

_____

_____

_____

_____

_____

_____

When a part of your mind tries to tell you that you were just imagining things or making it all up, tell that voice to "hush." Let yourself feel free to record any thoughts, feelings and beliefs, whether you know them to be real or you think they were imagined.

Let's take a journey through your life from birth to the present to see all the ways you've played out these thoughts and beliefs.

Ways these thoughts and beliefs have, and still are directing my life...

_____

_____

_____

_____

_____

The closer you come to knowing that you alone create the world of your experience, the more vital it becomes for you to discover just who is doing the creating.
— Eric Micha'el Leventhal

_____

_____

_____

_____

_____

_____

Now you have a clear picture of how your early beliefs and programming have affected your life. It's time to go back to the beginning and re-write your life script without the negative beliefs.

My New Life Script

_____

_____

Is your life story the truth? Yes, the chronological events are true. Is it the whole truth? No, you see and judge it through your conditioned eyes and mind – not of all involved – nor do you see the entire overview. Is it nothing but the truth? No, you select, share, delete, distort, subtract, assume and add what you want, need and choose to.
Rasheed Ogunlaru

_____

_____

_____

_____

_____

Become the loving, healing parent to the child who didn't know any better than to decide there must be something wrong with you. What does your child need to hear – want to hear?

_____

_____

_____

_____

_____

_____

_____

_____

_____

Hold yourself as a newborn infant in your arms and talk about your birth. Acknowledge her for the decisions made – tell her you know she was doing what she thought was best.

Listen – your child has a voice, and undoubtedly wants to talk to you. What does this child want to say to you? This is a powerful, healing moment for both of you.

_____

_____

_____

_____

_____

When you feel ready to go on, gently talk to you and your child. Have a conversation about the specifics of your birth and early childhood, and the story she made up about it.

_____

_____

_____

_____

_____

_____

_____

_____

Now, tell both of you the true story about who you really are and the beauty of your life.

_____

_____

_____

_____

_____

_____

_____

_____

_____

_____

From now on, whenever something happens to you that you wish hadn't -- stop and ask yourself,

"What must a person believe about themselves to have created this experience?"

I find it helpful to ask this question as if it is about someone else. This makes it much easier to be objective and explore the possibilities.

Our programming and thought patterns are deeply ingrained, and our responses to situations are most often automatic. You will find this is true even after you have re-written the script and created a new story. How many years have you spent seeing life this way?

Each time you do this process of changing your decisions and beliefs, you are peeling off another layer and bringing you closer to your heart.

Picture a meadow filled with tall grass. There are no paths across this meadow. The first time you walk through the grasses your footsteps leave a slight indentation, barely enough to find the path again. Then, as you walk the path over and over, the path becomes clearer and wider and easier to follow.

Eventually, it becomes your natural instinct to take this path across the meadow. For as long as it takes, patience is required to make a conscious choice over and over again to walk the new path until it becomes the automatic choice. And yes, sometimes it seems like it takes a very long time.

Disarming

My

Inner Critic

Disarming the critic is challenging when something happens or is said that triggers an unhealed spot inside you. Your goal is to stay *neutral* in the situation. I'll be the first to tell you that sometimes this seems to be an impossible goal. When you find yourself in reaction to a situation, it can feel like a moment of temporary insanity.

As stated in "A Course In Miracles," "I am never upset for the reason I think." Once the moment passes you are then able to be aware your reaction to the situation was compounded by the triggered unfelt pain of previous wounds.

In actuality the situation, or another person criticizing you, is a messenger sent from your *Higher Self*, God, The Universe, to help you find that unhealed place inside you. The truth is that everything someone says to you that causes a negative reaction is a mirror of what you are already saying to yourself. There are no exceptions here.

Just knowing this, however, isn't necessarily enough to keep you from reacting. Of course you're not going to feel like thanking them for the gift. You may feel more like retaliating and attacking them in return, which most likely would create a worse situation you would need to later repair.

A better idea is to come up with an action plan you can activate whenever you feel triggered by someone or a situation.

ACTION PLAN

I seriously need a speed bump between my brain and my mouth....!

1. *Take a deep breath. Release it slowly.*

2. *Say something like, "I need to think about this. I may or may not agree with you. Are you ok with me getting back to you later?"*

   Here's what I'll say _____

   _____

   _____

   _____

   This will accomplish two things: 1) The person who asks the question is always the person in control – you are no longer in defensive position, and 2) you can walk away without feeling like a victim and powerless.

3. As soon as possible get to a quiet place with pen and paper and write down what was said or what happened.

_____

_____

_____

_____

_____

_____

4. Write down what you are feeling and what it made you believe about you – use "I am" statements.

_____

_____

_____

_____

_____

The critical voices in our own heads are far more vicious than what we might hear from the outside. Our "inside critics" have intimate knowledge of us and can zero in on our weakest spots. S.A.R.K.

5. Journey back through your life until you come to the very first time you can remember thinking these thoughts and feeling these feelings. How old are you? _____

6. Ask your child to sit in your lap. Ask her to share her version of the story.

_____

_____

_____

_____

_____

_____

_____

7. As a loving parent, help your child unravel the lies in the story she created, and create a new story that is the truth about both of you.

_____

_____

_____

_____

_____

Remember, you have been criticizing yourself for years and it hasn't worked. Try approving of yourself and see what happens.
Louise Hay

_____

_____

_____

_____

_____

_____

_____

Disarming

My

Critical Parents

A roadblock you may run into when disarming the critic is concern about making your parents wrong because of things they said or did to you. It can be challenging to change your beliefs to something different than what you perceived your parents believed.

The truth is you do not need to make your parents wrong. What is helpful is to see them as people who made mistakes. If all of us on earth are here to learn and grow, it only makes sense that in the process of learning and growing we all sometimes miss the mark. This includes your parents.

Give yourself this gift -- take the time to do the following visualization of each of your parents. It will allow you to make a paradigm shift in your perception of them. It is powerful.

You will no doubt have to use your imagination, and then you'll wonder if you are just making it all up. It doesn't matter. What does matter is that you will be able to see and accept your parents as imperfect human beings. It will set you free from their beliefs, and make it possible for you to make different decisions about you and your life.

This process helps your child to know that how the "big people" are as adults is a result of what happened to them as children, and for sure, they make mistakes.

Father

Picture your father as you see him in present time with all his beliefs, characteristics and personality. Listen to his voice. What does it feel like to be in his presence? Focus on the aspects that have had a negative effect on your life.

_____

_____

_____

_____

_____

_____

Picture him as a little child. What does he look like, how does he sound? Feel him. Describe everything you see, hear and feel.

_____

_____

_____

_____

_____

_____

Look at his body language. Imagine what you think he believes about himself. Imagine his parents and what they might have said and taught your father. Ask yourself, "What must this child believe about himself and life to have been the kind of parent he is to me?"

_____

_____

_____

_____

_____

_____

_____

Visualize your father as he was growing up. See him as a teenager, then a young adult. What thoughts and beliefs might have determined the life path he chose to take?

Mother

Picture your mother as you see her in present time with all her beliefs, characteristics and personality. Listen to her voice. What does it feel like to be in her presence? Focus on the aspects that have had a negative effect on your life.

Picture her as a little child. What does she look like, how does she sound? Feel her. Describe everything you see, hear and feel.

_____

_____

_____

_____

_____

_____

_____

_____

Look at her body language. Imagine what you think she believes about herself. Imagine her parents and what they might have said and taught your mother. Ask, "What must she believe about herself and life to have been the kind of parent she is to me?"

_____

_____

_____

_____

_____

_____

Visualize your mother growing up. See her as a teenager, then as a young adult. What thoughts and beliefs might have determined the path she chose to take?

Fast Tract Program

For

Deactivating My Critic

Your Game Plan

1. *Make an agreement with yourself to become an acute observer of your thoughts. Start with a fifteen to twenty minute time span.*

2. *As a thought comes into your mind, push the pause button -- like you would on a recording.*

3. *Ask yourself where did this thought come from? Is it my thought? Or, is it someone else's thought that I've unknowingly accepted. Is this thought true, or have I been conditioned to believe it is true? Do I want to continue believing it, or would I rather choose another thought to replace it?*

4. *The more you practice this disarmament process the faster you become aware of each thought as it occurs and make a conscious choice to keep it or transform it.*

I don't want you to feel limited by which thoughts you can turn around and transform here. I know you have many, so you'll see there is a lot of space below to record and disarm many of your critical thoughts.

The Thought _____

Is it Mine or Another's? _____

Is it true? _____

Do I want to continue believing this thought or choose another?

_____

_____

_____

The Thought _____

Is it Mine or Another's? _____

Is it true? _____

Do I want to continue believing this thought or choose another?

_____

_____

_____

The Thought _____

Is it Mine or Another's? _____

Is it true? _____

Do I want to continue believing this thought or choose another?

_____

_____

_____

The Thought _____

Is it Mine or Another's? _____

Is it true? _____

Do I want to continue believing this thought or choose another?

_____

_____

_____

The Thought _____

Is it Mine or Another's? _____

Is it true? _____

Do I want to continue believing this thought or choose another?

_____

_____

_____

The Thought _____

Is it Mine or Another's? _____

Is it true? _____

Do I want to continue believing this thought or choose another?

_____

_____

_____

The Thought _____

Is it Mine or Another's? _____

Is it true? _____

Do I want to continue believing this thought or choose another?

_____

_____

_____

Emotional Giant

In Training

Do you really have to wait until you have healed every single wound, and hold only positive beliefs about you and your life, to experience the euphoria of *Emotional Giant* status? Or, is there a way you can make sure it is you *pulling your strings* instead of everyone else?

I found a shortcut that helped me bridge the gap between being in a state of reaction to other people's words, and being free from caring what anyone else thinks or says about me.

I am willing to be in a state
of self-acceptance
no matter what
I am experiencing

What would it look like if you accepted you even though you are imperfect? What do you do when someone makes a critical comment about you, and you feel like you've been stabbed with a knife, or even a little pin prick?

Here are 3 questions I ask that help me when I'm having a difficult moment. See if they help you to feel a little more like an Emotional Giant:

1. What is going on right now?

_____

_____

_____

_____

_____

2. Can I handle this?

_____

_____

_____

_____

_____

3. Am I willing to accept myself as I am in this moment? Be sure to include the child within you when you ask this question.

_____

The curious _____
paradox is that
when I accept _____
myself just as I
am, then I can _____
change. Carl Rogers

_____

_____

Once you acknowledge responsibility for your feelings when you feel criticized and do this healing work around it, you will be able to discover there is a second tier to achieving Emotional Giant status.

What you are going to do is take a cosmic point of view, seeing the totality of a situation -- the *big picture* of what is happening.

Pretend you are the director of a play -- you know all the players and their parts, and you understand how they all work together. When you are in the role of director it removes the possibility of allowing others to "pull your strings."

I can hear you asking, "why should I care about what was going on with anyone else? It's enough to figure out me." Yes, it is a lot to figure out yourself, and you are beginning to excel at just that. However, if you only look at what is happening with you, you'll miss half the gift the experience has the potential to give to you.

Remember, everything that happens outside of you is a mirror of something inside you. This means that whatever beliefs within this other person are causing them to judge/ criticize you are another aspect of this mirror.

It is so easy to be unaware of our self-judgements, and because of that we are unable to see the damage we are inflicting on ourselves because of them.

It took two years for me to figure out that a resentment I was holding against my sister for something she said about how I lived my life was actually a belief I was holding deep inside of me. When we are in denial about something it can be very elusive and difficult to uncover. Once I saw it, I realized how much damage it had been causing me.

We choose to be who we are, say what we say, do the things we do – and then we judge ourselves for our very beingness. How cruel we are to ourselves without even knowing it.

Are you feeling criticized by someone? Take some time to imagine what within them might be causing their need to be critical. What beliefs might be causing their judgment?

_____

_____

_____   *Don't criticize*

what you don't

_____   *understand,*

son. You never

_____   *walked in that*

man's shoes. —

_____   *Elvis Presley*

_____

Where is this belief inside me? How does this belief look/sound? What have I been secretly telling me about me?

_____

_____

_____

_____

_____

_____

_____

It is time to accept and forgive you. Are you ready? Write a note of forgiveness to you for judging you.

_____

_____

_____

The privilege of a lifetime is being who you are. —
Joseph Campbell
_____

_____

_____

_____

_____

Learning to Forgive

A Gift

I Give To Me

The act of forgiving has to begin with forgiving yourself. If forgiveness is not within you -- for you, then you do not have it within you to give to anyone else. If forgiving yourself seems impossible, then start with being *willing* to forgive yourself. Just being *willing* is enough to start the process.

As you begin forgiving and accepting yourself more, you will be amazed how it becomes easier and easier to accept and forgive others. The objective is that in time needing to forgive becomes a non-issue.

Here are 3 methods to engage the process of forgiving that I find are life-changing -- in fact almost miraculous in making forgiveness possible. My recommendation -- use them all.

Method 1 -- The Love Letter

The purpose for writing the Love Letter is to get out all the *stuff* that keeps you from feeling your love for someone, or even for yourself. The formula for the *Love Letter* comes from a book by Barbara DeAngelis, "How to Make Love the Rest of Your Life."

For forgiveness to occur, you must first start with forgiving yourself, so I recommend you write the first *Love Letter* to you. Don't be surprised if you find yourself writing many *Love Letters* to you. It is amazing how cleansing this process is.

This is a letter you may need to write many times to many people. There may be times you decide to share this letter with the intended recipient, or maybe never. It doesn't matter. It's all about the shift that happens within you in the writing.

Have an extra notepad nearby. Like me you may find yourself writing volumes, and may need even more space than provided to capture the feelings that spill out when your first start your letters. Don't limit yourself.

Writing a Love Letter is also helpful when you aren't sure what you are feeling, or you are afraid of your feelings once you do know what they are.

Dear _____

Something I am angry about is… it makes me mad when you…

_____

_____

_____

It hurts me when you... I feel sad because...

_____

_____

_____

_____

I am afraid that... It scares me when...

_____

_____

_____

_____

_____

_____

_____

_____

_____

_____

_____

_____

_____

Mardi Kirkland

_____

_____

_____

_____

_____

_____

What I could have done differently is... (Take responsibility for your part)

_____

_____

_____

_____

_____

_____

_____

_____

_____

_____

_____

_____

_____

_____

_____

_____

What I really want is... How I'd like it to be is...

_____

_____

_____

_____

_____

_____

_____

_____

_____

_____

_____

_____

_____

_____

_____

_____

What I love about you is...

_____

_____

_____

_____

_____

_____

_____

_____

_____

_____

_____

_____

_____

_____

_____

_____

Breathe

You may find it a huge struggle to forgive those whose words and actions have wounded you – especially when you were a child.

When you are tempted to hang on to your resentments, remember this – until you can forgive them, they still have control over you.

Method 2 -- Explore - What made them the way they are?

After writing *Love Letters*, your negative feelings towards those you want to forgive will undoubtedly be at least a bit neutralized. This is the time to journey again back into the childhood of the people you are finding it difficult to forgive.

Use your imagination. Write this out for each individual. There is space below for your mother and father, but you may have others that you'll want to do this for as well.

Mother

What was my mother taught by her parents?

_____

_____

_____

_____

_____

_____

_____

What decisions did she make about life as a result?

_____

_____

_____

_____

_____

_____

_____

How did this affect how she lived her life?

_____

_____

_____

_____

_____

_____

What did her childhood have to do with how she treated me?

_____

_____

_____

_____

_____

_____

_____

_____

_____

_____

"Imagining each of them in their childhood allowed me to change my perspective of them from being my attackers to seeing them as small, helpless children who were victims of how they were treated and what they were taught." — Who's Pulling My Strings

Father

What was my father taught by his parents?

_____

_____

_____

_____

_____

_____

What decisions did he make about life as a result?

_____

_____

_____

_____

_____

_____

_____

How did this affect how he lived his life?

_____

_____

_____

_____

_____

_____

_____

_____

What did his childhood have to do with how he treated me?

_____

_____

_____

_____

If they knew any better, they would act differently. They are not doing it "to you." They are doing it simply because that is what they know, and what they do.

_____

_____

_____

_____

_____

Hopefully, you are now able to see that in any given moment your mother and father, and anyone else who says critical words to you or gives you disapproving looks and actions, has only been acting from what they know -- their level of awareness. It is all about their perceptions and beliefs about life.

When you have the point of view that someone is doing something wrong that you need to forgive them for, it helps to stop reacting and ask a few questions:

What might be going on with this person right now that makes them act this way?

_____

_____

_____

_____

_____

_____

Where might they be hurting?

_____

_____

_____

_____

_____

What do they want that they're not getting?

_____

_____

_____

_____

_____

What do they really need from me?

_____

_____

_____

_____

_____

And, the most important question is…

What is unhealed in me that am I projecting on to them?

_____

_____

_____

Method 3 -- What if your entire life script is your design?

Being the creator you are -- this is a third way I suggest looking at your life – this one makes the need for forgiveness irrelevant.

If you are saying, "no way," I invite you to suspend your disbelief and let's consider the possibility – the positive *what ifs* -- knowing you are the *creator,* not the *victim* of your life.

Here's the premise – you had a purpose for coming into this life – something to master, something to teach, or perhaps a way to serve. Before we become physical beings in this earth life, we created the design of this life, as well as the other players to assist us on the journey of achieving our purpose.

What if?...

If the script for my life has been totally my creation, what might I have set it up to learn – to master – to teach through the experiences I've had?

_____

_____

_____

_____

_____

Ask yourself this question whenever even the littlest things occur in your day that are irritating. It makes it easy to let go and move forward.

Now -- these same people that were once on your *needing to* forgive list may move over to your gratitude list. Without them you might never have seen the hidden, unhealed parts that have kept you from loving and accepting you.

Let's make a "need to forgive" list and consider the purposes these people have served in your life.

NEED TO FORGIVE	GRATEFUL FOR
_____	_____
_____	_____
_____	_____
_____	_____
_____	_____
_____	_____

Person _____

Purpose served _____

_____

_____

Person _____

Purpose served _____

_____

_____

Person _____

Purpose served _____

_____

_____

Person _____

Purpose served _____

_____

_____

Person _____

Purpose served _____

_____

_____

Living Free

No Strings Attached!

Congratulations -- I am proud of you! You have been exploring, excavating and healing the beliefs and emotions that have kept you from feeling good, while working towards creating the life you want. Your perspective of you and life is definitely looking different than it was when you started.

This is not the end of the journey – this is just the beginning. Now Is the time to look forward. How good can your life get?

What is my dream – my vision for my life?

Take out your calendar and schedule time to imagine, to dream, to fantasize how you want your life to look, to feel, to be. When you do this and you dream dreams, receive images and receive inspiring ideas, I believe it is your Future Self beckoning to you.

I also believe there are vistas in the unlimited mind of God far beyond anything my finite mind can see.

Your Future Self is saying, "Keep going forward. No matter how hard the going gets, it is worth it – you are worth it! This dream is where your life is headed. Don't stop now."

One more tool – a Response Template

Before we go further into your messages from your Future Self, there is one more tool for your tool box that will be very helpful to have as you go forward.

It is inevitable, as you visualize, dream and plan, that you will discover more unhealed nooks and crannies inside you -- obstacles blocking your forward motion. You didn't really think you could do the processes in this book once and be done – did you? I wish that was true. The truth is that what you are becoming aware of, clearing and healing has been inside of you most of your life.

Anything you become aware of can be released and healed. Be willing to own that your thoughts and unresolved feelings are the creator of everything that shows up -- or doesn't show up in your life.

Lighten up ~ Be gentle with yourself!

You now have a satchel of tools to use whenever old conditioning or patterns get in your way. After doing this work for 30 years, I am still pulling out my journal and writing when an old pattern I had thought long ago healed rises up once again, and I feel stuck. It takes patience and commitment to yourself.

What about the situations and relationships where you find yourself going on *automatic pilot* – where you find you are reacting without thinking? It's ok – all of us experience this. What I find most helpful, knowing these moments will occur, is to *imagine* how you would respond if you were *aware* -- enlightened so to speak -- and didn't *react*.

The idea is to create *new templates* to be ready to use instead of your old *automatic responses*. This is another great opportunity to *play pretend* -- to have an imaginary conversation in your mind about the way you would like it to be. Imagine being sure of yourself, strong, and comfortable speaking your truth. Once you have a template implanted in your mind for how you want to be, it makes it possible for you to respond differently when the *trigger* moments occur.

CREATING NEW TEMPLATES

My Triggered Automatic Response _____

_____

_____

_____

My New Template to replace the old Automatic Response

_____

_____

_____

In that moment I understand that I have the power to create the situation right here, right now. I could walk past and say nothing, I could stop and talk, I could do whatever, and create a moment. Every moment is my moment to create.
Gregg Korrol

_____

_____

This I how I feel when I imagine responding with my new template

Don't believe what your eyes are telling you. All they show is limitation. Look with your understanding, find out what you already know, and you'll see the way to fly
  -Richard Bach

_____

_____

_____

_____

_____

What is my dream – for me, for my life, for the world?

Using pure imagination, dreams and fantasizing – allow your Future Self to reach back and talk to you.

This is my dream…

_____

_____

Without imagining a different world, you will keep creating more of the life you already have whether it is what you want or not.

_____

_____

_____

*Not to dream
boldly may turn
out to be
irresponsible.*
George Leonard

Make your life a Masterpiece; imagine no Limitations on what you Can be, have or do.
Brian Tracy

I dream of a world where there are no more puppets, and we are all free at last to live our lies with no strings attached. Oh Lord, I have a dream.
"Who's Pulling My Strings"

Printed in the United States
By Bookmasters